O'FLAHERTY V.C.

and

OVERRULED

By GEORGE BERNARD SHAW

A Digireads.com Book
Digireads.com Publishing

O'Flaherty V.C. and Overruled
By George Bernard Shaw
ISBN 10: 1-4209-4128-3
ISBN 13: 978-1-4209-4128-9

Please visit *www.digireads.com*

O'FLAHERTY V.C.

A RECRUITING PAMPHLET

At the door of an Irish country house in a park. Fine, summer weather; the summer of 1916. The porch, painted white, projects into the drive: but the door is at the side and the front has a window. The porch faces east: and the door is in the north side of it. On the south side is a tree in which a thrush is singing. Under the window is a garden seat with an iron chair at each end of it.

The last four bars of God Save the King are heard in the distance, followed by three cheers. Then the band strikes up It's a Long Way to Tipperary and recedes until it is out of hearing.

Private O'Flaherty V.C. comes wearily southward along the drive, and falls exhausted into the garden seat. The thrush utters a note of alarm and flies away. The tramp of a horse is heard.

A GENTLEMAN'S VOICE. Tim! Hi! Tim! [*He is heard dismounting.*]

A LABORER'S VOICE. Yes, your honor.

THE GENTLEMAN'S VOICE. Take this horse to the stables, will you?

A LABORER'S VOICE. Right, your honor. Yup there. Gwan now. Gwan. [*The horse is led away.*]

[*General Sir Pearce Madigan, an elderly baronet in khaki, beaming with enthusiasm, arrives. O'Flaherty rises and stands at attention.*]

SIR PEARCE. No, no, O'Flaherty: none of that now. You're off duty. Remember that though I am a general of forty years service, that little Cross of yours gives you a higher rank in the roll of glory than I can pretend to.

O'FLAHERTY [*relaxing.*] I'm thankful to you, Sir Pearce; but I wouldn't have anyone think that the baronet of my native place would let a common soldier like me sit down in his presence without leave.

SIR PEARCE. Well, you're not a common soldier, O'Flaherty: you're a very uncommon one; and I'm proud to have you for my guest here today.

O'FLAHERTY. Sure I know, sir. You have to put up with a lot from the like of me for the sake of the recruiting. All the quality shakes hands with me and says they're proud to know me, just the way the king said when he pinned the Cross on me. And it's as true as I'm standing here, sir, the queen said to me: "I hear you were born on the estate of General Madigan," she says; "and the General himself tells me you were always a fine young fellow." "Bedad, Mam," I says to her, "if the General knew all the rabbits I snared on him, and all the salmon I snatched on him, and all the cows I milked on him, he'd think me the finest ornament for the county jail he ever sent there for poaching."

SIR PEARCE [*Laughing.*] You're welcome to them all, my lad. Come [*he makes him sit down again on the garden seat*]! sit down and enjoy your holiday [*he sits down on one of the iron chairs; the one at the doorless side of the porch.*]

O'FLAHERTY. Holiday, is it? I'd give five shillings to be back in the trenches for the sake of a little rest and quiet. I never knew what hard work was till I took to recruiting. What with the standing on my legs all day, and the shaking hands, and the making speeches, and—what's worse—the listening to them and the calling for cheers for king and country, and the saluting the flag till I'm stiff with it, and the listening to them playing God Save the King and Tipperary, and the trying to make my eyes look moist like a man in a picture book, I'm that bet that I hardly get a wink of sleep. I give you my word, Sir Pearce, that I never heard the tune of Tipperary in my life till I came back from Flanders; and already it's drove me to that pitch of tiredness of it that when a poor little innocent slip of a boy in the street the other night drew himself up and saluted and began whistling it at me, I clouted his head for him, God forgive me.

SIR PEARCE [*soothingly.*] Yes, yes: I know. I know. One does get fed up with it: I've been dog tired myself on parade many a time. But still, you know, there's a gratifying side to it, too. After all, he is our king; and it's our own country, isn't it?

O'FLAHERTY. Well, sir, to you that have an estate in it, it would feel like your country. But the divil a perch of it ever I owned. And as to the king: God help him, my mother would have taken the skin off my back if I'd ever let on to have any other king than Parnell.

SIR PEARCE [*rising, painfully shocked.*] Your mother! What are you dreaming about, O'Flaherty? A most loyal woman. Always most loyal. Whenever there is an illness in the Royal Family, she asks me every time we meet about the health of the patient as anxiously as if it were yourself, her only son.

O'FLAHERTY. Well, she's my mother; and I won't utter a word agen her. But I'm not saying a word of lie when I tell you that that old woman is the biggest kanatt from here to the cross of Monasterboice. Sure she's the wildest Fenian and rebel, and always has been, that ever taught a poor innocent lad like myself to pray night and morning to St Patrick to clear the English out of Ireland the same as he cleared the snakes. You'll be surprised at my telling you that now, maybe, Sir Pearce?

SIR PEARCE [*unable to keep still, walking away from O'Flaherty.*] Surprised! I'm more than surprised, O'Flaherty. I'm overwhelmed. [*Turning and facing him.*] Are you—are you joking?

O'FLAHERTY. If you'd been brought up by my mother, sir, you'd know better than to joke about her. What I'm telling you is the truth; and I wouldn't tell it to you if I could see my way to get out of the fix I'll be in when my mother comes here this day to see her boy in his glory, and she after thinking all the time it was against the English I was fighting.

SIR PEARCE. Do you mean to say you told her such a monstrous falsehood as that you were fighting in the German army?

O'FLAHERTY. I never told her one word that wasn't the truth and nothing but the truth. I told her I was going to fight for the French and for the Russians; and sure who ever heard of the French or the Russians doing anything to the English but fighting them? That was how it was, sir. And sure the poor woman kissed me and went about the house singing in her old cracky voice that the French was on the sea, and they'd be here without delay, and the Orange will decay, says the Shan Van Vocht.

SIR PEARCE [*sitting down again, exhausted by his feelings.*] Well, I never could have believed this. Never. What do you suppose will happen when she finds out?

O'FLAHERTY. She mustn't find out. It's not that she'd half kill me, as big as I am and as brave as I am. It's that I'm fond of her, and can't bring myself to break the heart in her. You may think it queer that a man should be fond of his mother, sir, and she having bet him from the time he could feel to the time she was too slow to ketch him; but I'm fond of her; and I'm not ashamed of it. Besides, didn't she win the Cross for me?

SIR PEARCE. Your mother! How?

O'FLAHERTY. By bringing me up to be more afraid of running away than of fighting. I was timid by nature; and when the other boys hurted me, I'd want to run away and cry. But she whaled me for disgracing the blood of the O'Flahertys until I'd have fought the divil himself sooner than face her after funking a fight. That was how I got to know that fighting was easier than it looked, and that the others was as much afeard of me as I was of them, and that if I only held out long enough they'd lose heart and give rip. That's the way I came to be so courageous. I tell you, Sir Pearce, if the German army had been brought up by my mother, the Kaiser would be dining in the banqueting hall at Buckingham Palace this day, and King George polishing his jack boots for him in the scullery.

SIR PEARCE. But I don't like this, O'Flaherty. You can't go on deceiving your mother, you know. It's not right.

O'FLAHERTY. Can't go on deceiving her, can't I? It's little you know what a son's love can do, sir. Did you ever notice what a ready liar I am?

SIR PEARCE. Well, in recruiting a man gets carried away. I stretch it a bit occasionally myself. After all, it's for king and country. But if you won't mind my saying it, O'Flaherty, I think that story about your fighting the Kaiser and the twelve giants of the Prussian guard singlehanded would be the better for a little toning down. I don't ask you to drop it, you know; for it's popular, undoubtedly; but still, the truth is the truth. Don't you think it would fetch in almost as many recruits if you reduced the number of guardsmen to six?

O'FLAHERTY. You're not used to telling lies like I am, sir. I got great practice at home with my mother. What with saving my skin when I was young and thoughtless, and sparing her feelings when I was old enough to understand them, I've hardly told my mother the truth twice a year since I was born; and would you have me turn round on her and tell it now, when she's looking to have some peace and quiet in her old age?

SIR PEARCE [*troubled in his conscience.*] Well, it's not my affair, of course, O'Flaherty. But hadn't you better talk to Father Quinlan about it?

O'FLAHERTY. Talk to Father Quinlan, is it! Do you know what Father Quinlan says to me this very morning?

SIR PEARCE. Oh, you've seen him already, have you? What did he say?

O'FLAHERTY. He says "You know, don't you," he says, "that it's your duty, as a Christian and a good son of the Holy Church, to love your enemies?" he says. "I know it's my juty as a soldier to kill them," I says. "That's right, Dinny," he says: "quite right. But," says he, "you can kill them and do them a good turn afterward to show your love for them" he says; "and it's your duty to have a mass said for the souls of the hundreds of Germans you say you killed," says he; "for many and many of them were Bavarians and good Catholics," he says. "Is it me that must pay for masses for the souls of the Boshes?" I says. "Let the King of England pay for them," I says; "for it was his quarrel and not mine."

SIR PEARCE [*warmly.*] It is the quarrel of every honest man and true patriot, O'Flaherty. Your mother must see that as clearly as I do. After all, she is a reasonable, well disposed woman, quite capable of understanding the right and the wrong of the war. Why can't you explain to her what the war is about?

O'FLAHERTY. Arra, sir, how the divil do I know what the war is about?

SIR PEARCE [*rising again and standing over him.*] What! O'Flaherty: do you know what you are saying? You sit there wearing the Victoria Cross for having killed God knows how many Germans; and you tell me you don't know why you did it!

O'FLAHERTY. Asking your pardon, Sir Pearce, I tell you no such thing. I know quite well why I kilt them, because I was afeard that, if I didn't, they'd kill me.

SIR PEARCE [*giving it up, and sitting down again.*] Yes, yes, of course; but have you no knowledge of the causes of the war? of the interests at stake? of the importance—I may almost say—in fact I will say—the sacred right for which we are fighting? Don't you read the papers?

O'FLAHERTY. I do when I can get them. There's not many newsboys crying the evening paper in the trenches. They do say, Sir Pearce, that we shall never beat the Boshes until we make Horatio Bottomley Lord Leftnant of England. Do you think that's true, sir?

SIR PEARCE. Rubbish, man! there's no Lord Lieutenant in England: the king is Lord Lieutenant. It's a simple question of patriotism. Does patriotism mean nothing to you?

O'FLAHERTY. It means different to me than what it would to you, sir. It means England and England's king to you. To me and the like of me, it means talking about the English just the way the English papers talk about the Boshes. And what good has it ever done here in Ireland? It's kept me ignorant because it filled up my mother's mind, and she thought it ought to fill up mine too. It's kept Ireland poor, because instead of trying to better ourselves we thought we was the fine fellows of patriots when we were speaking evil of Englishmen that was as poor as ourselves and maybe as good as ourselves. The Boshes I kilt was more knowledgable men than me; and what better am I now that I've kilt them? What better is anybody?

SIR PEARCE [*huffed, turning a cold shoulder to him.*] I am sorry the terrible experience of this war—the greatest war ever fought—has taught you no better, O'Flaherty.

O'FLAHERTY [*preserving his dignity.*] I don't know about it's being a great war, sir. It's a big war; but that's not the same thing. Father Quinlan's new church is a big church: you might take the little old chapel out of the middle of it and not miss it. But my mother says there was more true religion in the old chapel. And the war has taught me that maybe she was right.

SIR PEARCE [*grunts sulkily*]!!

O'FLAHERTY [*respectfully but doggedly.*] And there's another thing it's taught me too, sir, that concerns you and me, if I may make bold to tell it to you.

SIR PEARCE [*still sulky.*] I hope it's nothing you oughtn't to say to me, O'Flaherty.

O'FLAHERTY. It's this, sir: that I'm able to sit here now and talk to you without humbugging you; and that's what not one of your tenants or your tenants' childer ever did to you before in all your long life. It's a true respect I'm showing you at last, sir. Maybe you'd rather have me humbug you and tell you lies as I used, just as the boys here, God help them, would rather have me tell them how I fought the Kaiser, that all the world knows I never saw in my life, than tell them the truth. But I can't take advantage of you the way I used, not even if I seem to be wanting in respect to you and cocked up by winning the Cross.

SIR PEARCE [*touched.*] Not at all, O'Flaherty. Not at all.

O'FLAHERTY. Sure what's the Cross to me, barring the little pension it carries? Do you think I don't know that there's hundreds of men as brave as me that never had the luck to get anything for their bravery but a curse from the sergeant, and the blame for the faults of them that ought to have been their betters? I've learnt more than you'd think, sir; for how would a gentleman like you know what a poor ignorant conceited creature I was when I went from here into the wide world as a soldier? What use is all the lying, and pretending, and humbugging, and letting on, when the day comes to you that your comrade is killed in the trench beside you, and you don't as much as look round at him until you trip over his poor body, and then all you say is to ask why the hell the stretcher-bearers don't take it out of the way. Why should I read the papers to be humbugged and lied to by them that had the cunning to stay at home and send me to fight for them? Don't talk to me or to any soldier of the war being right. No war is right; and all the holy water that Father Quinlan ever blessed couldn't make one right. There, sir! Now you know what O'Flaherty V.C. thinks; and you're wiser so than the others that only knows what he done.

SIR PEARCE [*making the best of it, and turning goodhumoredly to him again.*] Well, what you did was brave and manly, anyhow.

O'FLAHERTY. God knows whether it was or not, better than you nor me, General. I hope He won't be too hard on me for it, anyhow.

SIR PEARCE [*sympathetically.*] Oh yes: we all have to think seriously sometimes, especially when we're a little run down. I'm afraid we've been overworking you a bit over these recruiting meetings. However, we can knock off for the rest of the day; and tomorrow's Sunday. I've had about as much as I can stand myself. [*He looks at his watch.*] It's teatime. I wonder what's keeping your mother.

O'FLAHERTY. It's nicely cocked up the old woman will be having tea at the same table as you, sir, instead of in the kitchen. She'll be after dressing in the heighth of grandeur; and stop she will at every house on the way to show herself off and tell them where she's going, and fill the whole parish with spite and envy. But sure, she shouldn't keep you waiting, sir.

SIR PEARCE. Oh, that's all right: she must be indulged on an occasion like this. I'm sorry my wife is in London: she'd have been glad to welcome your mother.

O'FLAHERTY. Sure, I know she would, sir. She was always a kind friend to the poor. Little her ladyship knew, God help her, the depth of divilment that was in us: we were like a play to her. You see, sir, she was English: that was how it was. We was to her what the Pathans and Senegalese was to me when I first seen them: I couldn't think, somehow, that they were liars, and thieves, and backbiters, and drunkards, just like ourselves or any other Christians. Oh, her ladyship never knew all that was going on behind her back: how would she? When I was a weeshy child, she gave me the first penny I ever had in my hand; and I wanted to pray for her conversion that night the same as my mother made me pray for yours; and—

SIR PEARCE [*scandalized.*] Do you mean to say that your mother made you pray for MY conversion?

O'FLAHERTY. Sure and she wouldn't want to see a gentleman like you going to hell after she nursing your own son and bringing up my sister Annie on the bottle. That was how it was, sir. She'd rob you; and she'd lie to you; and she'd call down all the blessings of God on your head when she was selling you your own three geese that you thought had been ate by the fox the day after you'd finished fattening them, sir; and all the time you were like a bit of her own flesh and blood to her. Often has she said she'd live to see you a good Catholic yet, leading victorious armies against the

English and wearing the collar of gold that Malachi won from the proud invader. Oh, she's the romantic woman is my mother, and no mistake.

SIR PEARCE [*in great perturbation.*] I really can't believe this, O'Flaherty. I could have sworn your mother was as honest a woman as ever breathed.

O'FLAHERTY. And so she is, sir. She's as honest as the day.

SIR PEARCE. Do you call it honest to steal my geese?

O'FLAHERTY. She didn't steal them, sir. It was me that stole them.

SIR PEARCE. Oh! And why the devil did you steal them?

O'FLAHERTY. Sure we needed them, sir. Often and often we had to sell our own geese to pay you the rent to satisfy your needs; and why shouldn't we sell your geese to satisfy ours?

SIR PEARCE. Well, damn me!

O'FLAHERTY [*sweetly.*] Sure you had to get what you could out of us; and we had to get what we could out of you. God forgive us both!

SIR PEARCE. Really, O'Flaherty, the war seems to have upset you a little.

O'FLAHERTY. It's set me thinking, sir; and I'm not used to it. It's like the patriotism of the English. They never thought of being patriotic until the war broke out; and now the patriotism has took them so sudden and come so strange to them that they run about like frightened chickens, uttering all manner of nonsense. But please God they'll forget all about it when the war's over. They're getting tired of it already.

SIR PEARCE. No, no: it has uplifted us all in a wonderful way. The world will never be the same again, O'Flaherty. Not after a war like this.

O'FLAHERTY. So they all say, sir. I see no great differ myself. It's all the fright and the excitement; and when that quiets down they'll go back to their natural divilment and be the same as ever. It's like the vermin: it'll wash off after a while.

SIR PEARCE [*rising and planting himself firmly behind the garden seat.*] Well, the long and the short of it is, O'Flaherty, I must decline to be a party to any attempt to deceive your mother. I thoroughly disapprove of this feeling against the English, especially at a moment like the present. Even if your mother's political sympathies are really what you represent them to be, I should think that her gratitude to Gladstone ought to cure her of such disloyal prejudices.

O'FLAHERTY [*over his shoulder.*] She says Gladstone was an Irishman, Sir. What call would he have to meddle with Ireland as he did if he wasn't?

SIR PEARCE. What nonsense! Does she suppose Mr. Asquith is an Irishman?

O'FLAHERTY. She won't give him any credit for Home Rule, Sir. She says Redmond made him do it. She says you told her so.

SIR PEARCE [*convicted out of his own mouth.*] Well, I never meant her to take it up in that ridiculous way. [*He moves to the end of the garden seat on O'Flaherty's left.*] I'll give her a good talking to when she comes. I'm not going to stand any of her nonsense.

O'FLAHERTY. It's not a bit of use, sir. She says all the English generals is Irish. She says all the English poets and great men was Irish. She says the English never knew how to read their own books until we taught them. She says we're the lost tribes of the house of Israel and the chosen people of God. She says that the goddess Venus, that was born out of the foam of the sea, came up out of the water in Killiney Bay off Bray Head. She says that Moses built the seven churches, and that Lazarus was buried in Glasnevin.

SIR PEARCE. Bosh! How does she know he was? Did you ever ask her?

O'FLAHERTY. I did, sir, often.

SIR PEARCE. And what did she say?

O'FLAHERTY. She asked me how did I know he wasn't, and fetched me a clout on the side of my head.

SIR PEARCE. But have you never mentioned any famous Englishman to her, and asked her what she had to say about him?

O'FLAHERTY. The only one I could think of was Shakespeare, sir; and she says he was born in Cork.

SIR PEARCE [exhausted.] Well, I give it up [he throws himself into the nearest chair.] The woman is—Oh, well! No matter.

O'FLAHERTY [sympathetically.] Yes, sir: she's pigheaded and obstinate: there's no doubt about it. She's like the English: they think there's no one like themselves. It's the same with the Germans, though they're educated and ought to know better. You'll never have a quiet world till you knock the patriotism out of the human race.

SIR PEARCE. Still, we—

O'FLAHERTY. Whisht, sir, for God's sake: here she is.

The General jumps up. Mrs. O'Flaherty arrives and comes between the two men. She is very clean, and carefully dressed in the old fashioned peasant costume; black silk sunbonnet with a tiara of trimmings, and black cloak.

O'FLAHERTY [rising shyly.] Good evening, mother.

MRS. O'FLAHERTY [severely.] You hold your whisht, and learn behavior while I pay my juty to his honor. [To Sir Pearce, heartily.] And how is your honor's good self? And how is her ladyship and all the young ladies? Oh, it's right glad we are to see your honor back again and looking the picture of health.

SIR PEARCE [forcing a note of extreme geniality.] Thank you, Mrs. O'Flaherty. Well, you see we've brought you back your son safe and sound. I hope you're proud of him.

MRS. O'FLAHERTY. And indeed and I am, your honor. It's the brave boy he is; and why wouldn't he be, brought up on your honor's estate and with you before his eyes for a pattern of the finest soldier in Ireland. Come and kiss your old mother, Dinny darlint. [O'Flaherty does so sheepishly.] That's my own darling boy. And look at your fine new uniform stained already with the eggs you've been eating and the porter you've been drinking. [She takes out her handkerchief: spits on it: and scrubs his lapel with it.] Oh, it's the untidy slovenly one you always were. There! It won't be seen on the khaki: it's not like the old red coat that would show up everything that dribbled down on it. [To Sir Pearce.] And they tell me down at the lodge that her ladyship is staying in London, and that Miss Agnes is to be married to a fine young nobleman. Oh, it's your honor that is the lucky and happy father! It will be bad news for many of the young gentlemen of the quality round here, sir. There's lots thought she was going to marry young Master Lawless

SIR PEARCE. What! That—that—that bosthoon!

MRS. O'FLAHERTY [hilariously.] Let your honor alone for finding the right word! A big bosthoon he is indeed, your honor. Oh, to think of the times and times I have said that Miss Agnes would be my lady as her mother was before her! Didn't I, Dinny?

SIR PEARCE. And now, Mrs. O'Flaherty, I daresay you have a great deal to say to Dennis that doesn't concern me. I'll just go in and order tea.

MRS. O'FLAHERTY. Oh, why would your honor disturb yourself? Sure I can take the boy into the yard.

10

SIR PEARCE. Not at all. It won't disturb me in the least. And he's too big a boy to be taken into the yard now. He has made a front seat for himself. Eh? [*He goes into the house.*]

MRS. O'FLAHERTY. Sure he has that, your honor. God bless your honor! [*The General being now out of hearing, she turns threateningly to her son with one of those sudden Irish changes of manner which amaze and scandalize less flexible nations, and exclaims.*] And what do you mean, you lying young scald, by telling me you were going to fight agen the English? Did you take me for a fool that couldn't find out, and the papers all full of you shaking hands with the English king at Buckingham Palace?

O'FLAHERTY. I didn't shake hands with him: he shook hands with me. Could I turn on the man in his own house, before his own wife, with his money in my pocket and in yours, and throw his civility back in his face?

MRS. O'FLAHERTY. You would take the hand of a tyrant red with the blood of Ireland—

O'FLAHERTY. Arra hold your nonsense, mother: he's not half the tyrant you are, God help him. His hand was cleaner than mine that had the blood of his own relations on it, maybe.

MRS. O'FLAHERTY [*threateningly.*] Is that a way to speak to your mother, you young spalpeen?

O'FLAHERTY [*stoutly.*] It is so, if you won't talk sense to me. It's a nice thing for a poor boy to be made much of by kings and queens, and shook hands with by the heighth of his country's nobility in the capital cities of the world, and then to come home and be scolded and insulted by his own mother. I'll fight for who I like; and I'll shake hands with what kings I like; and if your own son is not good enough for you, you can go and look for another. Do you mind me now?

MRS. O'FLAHERTY. And was it the Belgians learned you such brazen impudence?

O'FLAHERTY. The Belgians is good men; and the French ought to be more civil to them, let alone their being half murdered by the Boshes.

MRS. O'FLAHERTY. Good men is it! Good men! to come over here when they were wounded because it was a Catholic country, and then to go to the Protestant Church because it didn't cost them anything, and some of them to never go near a church at all. That's what you call good men!

O'FLAHERTY. Oh, you're the mighty fine politician, aren't you? Much you know about Belgians or foreign parts or the world you're living in, God help you!

MRS. O'FLAHERTY. Why wouldn't I know better than you? Amment I your mother?

O'FLAHERTY. And if you are itself, how can you know what you never seen as well as me that was dug into the continent of Europe for six months, and was buried in the earth of it three times with the shells bursting on the top of me? I tell you I know what I'm about. I have my own reasons for taking part in this great conflict. I'd be ashamed to stay at home and not fight when everybody else is fighting.

MRS. O'FLAHERTY. If you wanted to fight, why couldn't you fight in the German army?

O'FLAHERTY. Because they only get a penny a day.

MRS. O'FLAHERTY. Well, and if they do itself, isn't there the French army?

O'FLAHERTY. They only get a hapenny a day.

MRS. O'FLAHERTY [*much dashed.*] Oh murder! They must be a mean lot, Dinny.

O'FLAHERTY [*sarcastic.*] Maybe you'd have me in the Turkish army, and worship the heathen Mahomet that put a corn in his ear and pretended it was a message from the heavens when the pigeon come to pick it out and eat it. I went where I could get the biggest allowance for you; and little thanks I get for it!

MRS. O'FLAHERTY. Allowance, is it! Do you know what the thieving blackguards did on me? They came to me and they says, "Was your son a big eater?" they says. "Oh, he was that," says I: "ten shillings a week wouldn't keep him." Sure I thought the more I said the more they'd give me. "Then," says they, "that's ten shillings a week off your allowance," they says, "because you save that by the king feeding him." "Indeed!" says I: "I suppose if I'd six sons, you'd stop three pound a week from me, and make out that I ought to pay you money instead of you paying me." "There's a fallacy in your argument," they says.

O'FLAHERTY. A what?

MRS. O'FLAHERTY. A fallacy: that's the word he said. I says to him, "It's a Pharisee I'm thinking you mean, sir; but you can keep your dirty money that your king grudges a poor old widow; and please God the English will be got yet for the deadly sin of oppressing the poor;" and with that I shut the door in his face.

O'FLAHERTY [*furious.*] Do you tell me they knocked ten shillings off you for my keep?

MRS. O'FLAHERTY [*soothing him.*] No, darlint: they only knocked off half a crown. I put up with it because I've got the old age pension; and they know very well I'm only sixty-two; so I've the better of them by half a crown a week anyhow.

O'FLAHERTY. It's a queer way of doing business. If they'd tell you straight out what they was going to give you, you wouldn't mind; but if there was twenty ways of telling the truth and only one way of telling a lie, the Government would find it out. It's in the nature of governments to tell lies.

Teresa Driscoll, a parlor maid, comes from the house,

TERESA. You're to come up to the drawing-room to have your tea, Mrs. O'Flaherty.

MRS. O'FLAHERTY. Mind you have a sup of good black tea for me in the kitchen afterwards, acushla. That washy drawing-room tea will give me the wind if I leave it on my stomach. [*She goes into the house, leaving the two young people alone together.*]

O'FLAHERTY. Is that yourself, Tessie? And how are you?

TERESA. Nicely, thank you. And how's yourself?

O'FLAHERTY. Finely, thank God. [*He produces a gold chain.*] Look what I've brought you, Tessie.

TERESA [*shrinking.*] Sure I don't like to touch it, Denny. Did you take it off a dead man?

O'FLAHERTY. No: I took it off a live one; and thankful he was to me to be alive and kept a prisoner in ease and comfort, and me left fighting in peril of my life.

TERESA [*taking it.*] Do you think it's real gold, Denny?

O'FLAHERTY. It's real German gold, anyhow.

TERESA. But German silver isn't real, Denny.

O'FLAHERTY [*his face darkening.*] Well, it's the best the Bosh could do for me, anyhow.

TERESA. Do you think I might take it to the jeweller next market day and ask him?

O'FLAHERTY [*sulkily.*] You may take it to the divil if you like.

TERESA. You needn't lose your temper about it. I only thought I'd like to know. The nice fool I'd look if I went about showing off a chain that turned out to be only brass!

O'FLAHERTY. I think you might say Thank you.

TERESA. Do you? I think you might have said something more to me than "Is that yourself?" You couldn't say less to the postman.

O'FLAHERTY [*his brow clearing.*] Oh, is that what's the matter? Here! come and take the taste of ther brass out of my mouth. [*He seizes her and kisses her.*]

[*Teresa, without losing her Irish dignity, takes the kiss as appreciatively as a connoisseur might take a glass of wine, and sits down with him on the garden seat.*]

TERESA [*as he squeezes her waist.*] Thank God the priest can't see us here!

O'FLAHERTY. It's little they care for priests in France, alanna.

TERESA. And what had the queen on her, Denny, when she spoke to you in the palace?

O'FLAHERTY. She had a bonnet on without any strings to it. And she had a plakeen of embroidery down her bosom. And she had her waist where it used to be, and not where the other ladies had it. And she had little brooches in her ears, though she hadn't half the jewelry of Mrs. Sullivan that keeps the popshop in Drumpogue. And she dresses her hair down over her forehead, in a fringe like. And she has an Irish look about her eyebrows. And she didn't know what to say to me, poor woman! and I didn't know what to say to her, God help me!

TERESA. You'll have a pension now with the Cross, won't you, Denny?

O'FLAHERTY. Sixpence three farthings a day.

TERESA. That isn't much.

O'FLAHERTY. I take out the rest in glory.

TERESA. And if you're wounded, you'll have a wound pension, won't you?

O'FLAHERTY. I will, please God.

TERESA. You're going out again, aren't you, Denny?

O'FLAHERTY. I can't help myself. I'd be shot for a deserter if I didn't go; and maybe I'll be shot by the Boshes if I do go; so between the two of them I'm nicely fixed up.

MRS. O'FLAHERTY [*calling from within the house.*] Tessie! Tessie darlint!

TERESA [*disengaging herself from his arm and rising.*] I'm wanted for the tea table. You'll have a pension anyhow, Denny, won't you, whether you're wounded or not?

MRS. O'FLAHERTY. Come, child, come.

TERESA [*impatiently.*] Oh, sure I'm coming. [*She tries to smile at Denny, not very convincingly, and hurries into the house.*]

O'FLAHERTY [*alone.*] And if I do get a pension itself, the divil a penny of it you'll ever have the spending of.

MRS. O'FLAHERTY [*as she comes from the porch.*] Oh, it's a shame for you to keep the girl from her juties, Dinny. You might get her into trouble.

O'FLAHERTY. Much I care whether she gets into trouble or not! I pity the man that gets her into trouble. He'll get himself into worse.

MRS. O'FLAHERTY. What's that you tell me? Have you been falling out with her, and she a girl with a fortune of ten pounds?

O'FLAHERTY. Let her keep her fortune. I wouldn't touch her with the tongs if she had thousands and millions.

MRS. O'FLAHERTY. Oh fie for shame, Dinny! why would you say the like of that of a decent honest girl, and one of the Driscolls too?

O'FLAHERTY. Why wouldn't I say it? She's thinking of nothing but to get me out there again to be wounded so that she may spend my pension, bad scran to her!

MRS. O'FLAHERTY. Why, what's come over you, child, at all at all?

O'FLAHERTY. Knowledge and wisdom has come over me with pain and fear and trouble. I've been made a fool of and imposed upon all my life. I thought that covetious sthreal in there was a walking angel; and now if ever I marry at all I'll marry a Frenchwoman.

MRS. O'FLARERTY [*fiercely.*] You'll not, so; and don't you dar repeat such a thing to me.

O'FLAHERTY. Won't I, faith! I've been as good as married to a couple of them already.

MRS. O'FLAHERTY. The Lord be praised, what wickedness have you been up to, you young blackguard?

O'FLAHERTY. One of them Frenchwomen would cook you a meal twice in the day and all days and every day that Sir Pearce himself might go begging through Ireland for, and never see the like of. I'll have a French wife, I tell you; and when I settle down to be a farmer I'll have a French farm, with a field as big as the continent of Europe that ten of your dirty little fields here wouldn't so much as fill the ditch of.

MRS. O'FLAHERTY [*furious.*] Then it's a French mother you may go look for; for I'm done with you.

O'FLAHERTY. And it's no great loss you'd be if it wasn't for my natural feelings for you; for it's only a silly ignorant old countrywoman you are with all your fine talk about Ireland: you that never stepped beyond the few acres of it you were born on!

MRS. O'FLAHERTY [*tottering to the garden seat and showing signs of breaking down.*] Dinny darlint, why are you like this to me? What's happened to you?

O'FLAHERTY [*gloomily.*] What's happened to everybody? that's what I want to know. What's happened to you that I thought all the world of and was afeard of? What's happened to Sir Pearce, that I thought was a great general, and that I now see to be no more fit to command an army than an old hen? What's happened to Tessie, that I was mad to marry a year ago, and that I wouldn't take now with all Ireland for her fortune? I tell you the world's creation is crumbling in ruins about me; and then you come and ask what's happened to me?

MRS. O'FLAHERTY [*giving way to wild grief.*] Ochone! ochone! my son's turned agen me. Oh, what'll I do at all at all? Oh! oh! oh! oh!

SIR PEARCE [*running out of the house.*] What's this infernal noise? What on earth is the matter?

O'FLAHERTY. Arra hold your whisht, mother. Don't you see his honor?

MRS. O'FLAHERTY. Oh, Sir, I'm ruined and destroyed. Oh, won't you speak to Dinny, Sir: I'm heart scalded with him. He wants to marry a Frenchwoman on me, and to go away and be a foreigner and desert his mother and betray his country. It's mad he is with the roaring of the cannons and he killing the Germans and the Germans killing him, bad cess to them! My boy is taken from me and turned agen me; and who is to take care of me in my old age after all I've done for him, ochone! ochone!

O'FLAHERTY. Hold your noise, I tell you. Who's going to leave you? I'm going to take you with me. There now: does that satisfy you?

MRS. O'FLAHERTY. Is it take me into a strange land among heathens and pagans and savages, and me not knowing a word of their language nor them of mine?

O'FLAHERTY. A good job they don't: maybe they'll think you're talking sense.

MRS. O'FLAHERTY. Ask me to die out of Ireland, is it? and the angels not to find me when they come for me!

O'FLAHERTY. And would you ask me to live in Ireland where I've been imposed on and kept in ignorance, and to die where the divil himself wouldn't take me as a gift, let alone the blessed angels? You can come or stay. You can take your old way or take my young way. But stick in this place I will not among a lot of good-for-nothing divils that'll not do a hand's turn but watch the grass growing and build up the stone wall where the cow walked through it. And Sir Horace Plunkett breaking his heart all the time telling them how they might put the land into decent tillage like the French and Belgians.

SIR PEARCE. Yes, he's quite right, you know, Mrs. O'Flaherty: quite right there.

MRS. O'FLAHERTY. Well, sir, please God the war will last a long time yet; and maybe I'll die before it's over and the separation allowance stops.

O'FLAHERTY. That's all you care about. It's nothing but milch cows we men are for the women, with their separation allowances, ever since the war began, bad luck to them that made it!

TERESA [*coming from the porch between the General and Mrs. O'Flaherty.*] Hannah sent me out for to tell you, sir, that the tea will be black and the cake not fit to eat with the cold if yous all don't come at wanst.

MRS. O'FLAHERTY [*breaking out again.*] Oh, Tessie darlint, what have you been saying to Dinny at all at all? Oh! Oh—

SIR PEARCE [*out of patience.*] You can't discuss that here. We shall have Tessie beginning now.

O'FLAHERTY. That's right, sir: drive them in.

TERESA. I haven't said a word to him. He—

SIR PEARCE. Hold your tongue; and go in and attend to your business at the tea table.

TERESA. But amment I telling your honor that I never said a word to him? He gave me a beautiful gold chain. Here it is to show your honor that it's no lie I'm telling you.

SIR PEARCE. What's this, O'Flaherty? You've been looting some unfortunate officer.

O'FLAHERTY. No, sir: I stole it from him of his own accord.

MRS. O'FLAHERTY. Wouldn't your honor tell him that his mother has the first call on it? What would a slip of a girl like that be doing with a gold chain round her neck?

TERESA [*venomously.*] Anyhow, I have a neck to put it round and not a hank of wrinkles.

[*At this unfortunate remark, Mrs. O'Flaherty bounds from her seat: and an appalling tempest of wordy wrath breaks out. The remonstrances and commands of the General, and the protests and menaces of O'Flaherty, only increase the hubbub. They are soon all speaking at once at the top of their voices.*]

MRS. O'FLAHERTY [*solo.*] You impudent young heifer, how dar you say such a thing to me? [*Teresa retorts furiously: the men interfere: and the solo becomes a quartet, fortissimo.*] I've a good mind to clout your ears for you to teach you manners. Be ashamed of yourself, do; and learn to know who you're speaking to. That I maytn't sin! but I don't know what the good God was thinking about when he made the like of you. Let me not see you casting sheep's eyes at my son again. There never was an O'Flaherty yet that would demean himself by keeping company with a dirty Driscoll; and if I see you next or nigh my house I'll put you in the ditch with a flea in your ear: mind that now.

TERESA. Is it me you offer such a name to, you fou-mouthed, dirty-minded, lying, sloothering old sow, you? I wouldn't soil my tongue by calling you in your right name and telling Sir Pearce what's the common talk of the town about you. You and your O'Flahertys! setting yourself up agen the Driscolls that would never lower themselves to be seen in conversation with you at the fair. You can keep your ugly stingy lump of a son; for what is he but a common soldier? and God help the girl that gets him, say I! So the back of my hand to you, Mrs. O'Flaherty; and that the cat may tear your ugly old face!

SIR PEARCE. Silence. Tessie, did you hear me ordering you to go into the house? Mrs. O'Flaherty! [*Louder.*] Mrs. O'Flaherty!! Will you just listen to me one moment? Please. [*Furiously.*] Do you hear me speaking to you, woman? Are you human beings or are you wild beasts? Stop that noise immediately: do you hear? [*Yelling.*] Are you going to do what I order you, or are you not? Scandalous! Disgraceful! This comes of being too familiar with you. O'Flaherty, shove them into the house. Out with the whole damned pack of you.

O'FLAHERTY [*to the women.*] Here now: none of that, none of that. Go easy, I tell you. Hold your whisht, mother, will you, or you'll be sorry for it after. [*To Teresa.*] Is that the way for a decent young girl to speak? [*Despairingly.*] Oh, for the Lord's sake, shut up, will yous? Have you no respect for yourselves or your betters? [*Peremptorily.*] Let me have no more of it, I tell you. Och! the divil's in the whole crew of you. In with you into the house this very minute and tear one another's eyes out in the kitchen if you like. In with you.

[*The two men seize the two women, and push them, still violently abusing one another, into the house. Sir Pearce slams the door upon them savagely. Immediately a heavenly silence falls on the summer afternoon. The two sit down out of breath: and for a long time nothing is said. Sir Pearce sits on an iron chair. O'Flaherty sits on the garden seat. The thrush begins to sing melodiously. O'Flaherty cocks his ears, and looks up at it. A smile spreads over his troubled features. Sir Pearce, with a long sigh, takes out his pipe and begins to fill it.*]

O'FLAHERTY [*idyllically.*] What a discontented sort of an animal a man is, sir! Only a month ago, I was in the quiet of the country out at the front, with not a sound except the birds and the bellow of a cow in the distance as it might be, and the shrapnel making little clouds in the heavens, and the shells whistling, and maybe a yell or two when one of us was hit; and would you believe it, sir, I complained of the noise and wanted to have a peaceful hour at home. Well: them two has taught me a lesson. This morning, sir, when I was telling the boys here how I was longing to be back taking my part for king and country with the others, I was lying, as you well knew, sir. Now I can go and say it with a clear conscience. Some likes war's alarums; and some likes home life. I've tried both, sir; and I'm for war's alarums now. I always was a quiet lad by natural disposition.

SIR PEARCE. Strictly between ourselves, O'Flaherty, and as one soldier to another [*O'Flaherty salutes, but without stiffening*], do you think we should have got an army without conscription if domestic life had been as happy as people say it is?

O'FLAHERTY. Well, between you and me and the wall, Sir Pearce, I think the less we say about that until the war's over, the better.

[*He winks at the General. The General strikes a match. The thrush sings. A jay laughs. The conversation drops.*]

OVERRULED

A lady and gentleman are sitting together on a chesterfield in a retired corner of the lounge of a seaside hotel. It is a summer night: the French window behind them stands open. The terrace without overlooks a moonlit harbor. The lounge is dark. The chesterfield, upholstered in silver grey, and the two figures on it in evening dress, catch the light from an arc lamp somewhere; but the walls, covered with a dark green paper, are in gloom. There are two stray chairs, one on each side. On the gentleman's right, behind him up near the window, is an unused fireplace. Opposite it on the lady's left is a door. The gentleman is on the lady's right.

The lady is very attractive, with a musical voice and soft appealing manners. She is young: that is, one feels sure that she is under thirty-five and over twenty-four. The gentleman does not look much older. He is rather handsome, and has ventured as far in the direction of poetic dandyism in the arrangement of his hair as any man who is not a professional artist can afford to in England. He is obviously very much in love with the lady, and is, in fact, yielding to an irresistible impulse to throw his arms around her.

THE LADY. Don't—oh don't be horrid. Please, Mr. Lunn [*she rises from the lounge and retreats behind it*]! Promise me you won't be horrid.

GREGORY. LUNN. I'm not being horrid, Mrs. Juno. I'm not going to be horrid. I love you: that's all. I'm extraordinarily happy.

MRS. JUNO. You will really be good?

GREGORY. I'll be whatever you wish me to be. I tell you I love you. I love loving you. I don't want to be tired and sorry, as I should be if I were to be horrid. I don't want you to be tired and sorry. Do come and sit down again.

MRS. JUNO. [*coming back to her seat.*] You're sure you don't want anything you oughtn't to?

GREGORY. Quite sure. I only want you [*she recoils.*] Don't be alarmed. I like wanting you. As long as I have a want, I have a reason for living. Satisfaction is death.

MRS. JUNO. Yes; but the impulse to commit suicide is sometimes irresistible.

GREGORY. Not with you.

MRS. JUNO. What!

GREGORY. Oh, it sounds uncomplimentary; but it isn't really. Do you know why half the couples who find themselves situated as we are now behave horridly?

MRS. JUNO. Because they can't help it if they let things go too far.

GREGORY. Not a bit of it. It's because they have nothing else to do, and no other way of entertaining each other. You don't know what it is to be alone with a woman who has little beauty and less conversation. What is a man to do? She can't talk interestingly; and if he talks that way himself she doesn't understand him. He can't look at her: if he does, he only finds out that she isn't beautiful. Before the end of five minutes they are both hideously bored. There's only one thing that can save the situation; and that's what you call being horrid. With a beautiful, witty, kind woman, there's no time for such follies. It's so delightful to look at her, to listen to her voice, to hear all she has to say, that nothing else happens. That is why the woman who is supposed to have a thousand lovers seldom has one; whilst the stupid, graceless animals of women have dozens.

MRS. JUNO. I wonder! It's quite true that when one feels in danger one talks like mad to stave it off, even when one doesn't quite want to stave it off.

GREGORY. One never does quite want to stave it off. Danger is delicious. But death isn't. We court the danger; but the real delight is in escaping, after all.

MRS. JUNO. I don't think we'll talk about it any more. Danger is all very well when you do escape; but sometimes one doesn't. I tell you frankly I don't feel as safe as you do—if you really do.

GREGORY. But surely you can do as you please without injuring anyone, Mrs. Juno. That is the whole secret of your extraordinary charm for me.

MRS. JUNO. I don't understand.

GREGORY. Well, I hardly know how to begin to explain. But the root of the matter is that I am what people call a good man.

MRS. JUNO. I thought so until you began making love to me.

GREGORY. But you knew I loved you all along.

MRS. JUNO. Yes, of course; but I depended on you not to tell me so; because I thought you were good. Your blurting it out spoilt it. And it was wicked besides.

GREGORY. Not at all. You see, it's a great many years since I've been able to allow myself to fall in love. I know lots of charming women; but the worst of it is, they're all married. Women don't become charming, to my taste, until they're fully developed; and by that time, if they're really nice, they're snapped up and married. And then, because I am a good man, I have to place a limit to my regard for them. I may be fortunate enough to gain friendship and even very warm affection from them; but my loyalty to their husbands and their hearths and their happiness obliges me to draw a line and not overstep it. Of course I value such affectionate regard very highly indeed. I am surrounded with women who are most dear to me. But every one of them has a post sticking up, if I may put it that way, with the inscription Trespassers Will Be Prosecuted. How we all loathe that notice! In every lovely garden, in every dell full of primroses, on every fair hillside, we meet that confounded board; and there is always a gamekeeper round the corner. But what is that to the horror of meeting it on every beautiful woman, and knowing that there is a husband round the corner? I have had this accursed board standing between me and every dear and desirable woman until I thought I had lost the power of letting myself fall really and wholeheartedly in love.

MRS. JUNO. Wasn't there a widow?

GREGORY. No. Widows are extraordinarily scarce in modern society. Husbands live longer than they used to; and even when they do die, their widows have a string of names down for their next.

MRS. JUNO. Well, what about the young girls?

GREGORY. Oh, who cares for young girls? They're sympathetic. They're beginners. They don't attract me. I'm afraid of them.

MRS. JUNO. That's the correct thing to say to a woman of my age. But it doesn't explain why you seem to have put your scruples in your pocket when you met me.

GREGORY. Surely that's quite clear. I—

MRS. JUNO. No: please don't explain. I don't want to know. I take your word for it. Besides, it doesn't matter now. Our voyage is over; and to-morrow I start for the north to my poor father's place.

GREGORY. [surprised.] Your poor father! I thought he was alive.

MRS. JUNO. So he is. What made you think he wasn't?

GREGORY. You said your POOR father.

MRS. JUNO. Oh, that's a trick of mine. Rather a silly trick, I Suppose; but there's something pathetic to me about men: I find myself calling them poor So-and-So when there's nothing whatever the matter with them.

GREGORY. [*who has listened in growing alarm.*] But—I—is?—wa—? Oh, Lord!

MRS. JUNO. What's the matter?

GREGORY. Nothing.

MRS. JUNO. Nothing! [*Rising anxiously.*] Nonsense: you're ill.

GREGORY. No. It was something about your late husband—

MRS. JUNO. My LATE husband! What do you mean? [*clutching him, horror-stricken.*] Don't tell me he's dead.

GREGORY. [*rising, equally appalled.*] Don't tell me he's alive.

MRS. JUNO. Oh, don't frighten me like this. Of course he's alive—unless you've heard anything.

GREGORY. The first day we met—on the boat—you spoke to me of your poor dear husband.

MRS. JUNO. [*releasing him, quite reassured.*] Is that all?

GREGORY. Well, afterwards you called him poor Tops. Always poor Tops, Our poor dear Tops. What could I think?

MRS. JUNO. [*sitting down again.*] I wish you hadn't given me such a shock about him; for I haven't been treating him at all well. Neither have you.

GREGORY. [*relapsing into his seat, overwhelmed.*] And you mean to tell me you're not a widow!

MRS. JUNO. Gracious, no! I'm not in black.

GREGORY. Then I have been behaving like a blackguard. I have broken my promise to my mother. I shall never have an easy conscience again.

MRS. JUNO. I'm sorry. I thought you knew.

GREGORY. You thought I was a libertine?

MRS. JUNO. No: of course I shouldn't have spoken to you if I had thought that. I thought you liked me, but that you knew, and would be good.

GREGORY. [*stretching his hands towards her breast.*] I thought the burden of being good had fallen from my soul at last. I saw nothing there but a bosom to rest on: the bosom of a lovely woman of whom I could dream without guilt. What do I see now?

MRS. JUNO. Just what you saw before.

GREGORY. [*despairingly.*] No, no.

MRS. JUNO. What else?

GREGORY. Trespassers Will Be Prosecuted: Trespassers Will Be Prosecuted.

MRS. JUNO. They won't if they hold their tongues. Don't be such a coward. My husband won't eat you.

GREGORY. I'm not afraid of your husband. I'm afraid of my conscience.

MRS. JUNO. [*losing patience.*] Well! I don't consider myself at all a badly behaved woman; for nothing has passed between us that was not perfectly nice and friendly; but really! to hear a grown-up man talking about promises to his mother!

GREGORY. [*interrupting her.*] Yes, Yes: I know all about that. It's not romantic: it's not Don Juan: it's not advanced; but we feel it all the same. It's far deeper in our blood and bones than all the romantic stuff. My father got into a scandal once: that was why my mother made me promise never to make love to a married woman. And now I've done it I can't feel honest. Don't pretend to despise me or laugh at me. You feel it too. You said just now that your own conscience was uneasy when you thought of your husband. What must it be when you think of my wife?

MRS. JUNO. [*rising aghast.*] Your wife!!! You don't dare sit there and tell me coolly that you're a married man!

GREGORY. I never led you to believe I was unmarried.

MRS. JUNO. Oh! You never gave me the faintest hint that you had a wife.

GREGORY. I did indeed. I discussed things with you that only married people really understand.

MRS. JUNO. Oh!!

GREGORY. I thought it the most delicate way of letting you know.

MRS. JUNO. Well, you ARE a daisy, I must say. I suppose that's vulgar; but really! really!! You and your goodness! However, now we've found one another out there's only one thing to be done. Will you please go?

GREGORY. [*rising slowly.*] I OUGHT to go.

MRS. JUNO. Well, go.

GREGORY. Yes. Er—[*he tries to go.*] I—I somehow can't. [*He sits down again helplessly.*] My conscience is active: my will is paralyzed. This is really dreadful. Would you mind ringing the bell and asking them to throw me out? You ought to, you know.

MRS. JUNO. What! make a scandal in the face of the whole hotel! Certainly not. Don't be a fool.

GREGORY. Yes; but I can't go.

MRS. JUNO. Then I can. Goodbye.

GREGORY. [*clinging to her hand.*] Can you really?

MRS. JUNO. Of course I—[*she wavers.*] Oh, dear! [*They contemplate one another helplessly.*] I can't. [*She sinks on the lounge, hand in hand with him.*]

GREGORY. For heaven's sake pull yourself together. It's a question of self-control.

MRS. JUNO. [*dragging her hand away and retreating to the end of the chesterfield.*] No: it's a question of distance. Self-control is all very well two or three yards off, or on a ship, with everybody looking on. Don't come any nearer.

GREGORY. This is a ghastly business. I want to go away; and I can't.

MRS. JUNO. I think you ought to go [*he makes an effort; and she adds quickly*] but if you try I shall grab you round the neck and disgrace myself. I implore you to sit still and be nice.

GREGORY. I implore you to run away. I believe I can trust myself to let you go for your own sake. But it will break my heart.

MRS. JUNO. I don't want to break your heart. I can't bear to think of your sitting here alone. I can't bear to think of sitting alone myself somewhere else. It's so senseless—so ridiculous—when we might be so happy. I don't want to be wicked, or coarse. But I like you very much; and I do want to be affectionate and human.

GREGORY. I ought to draw a line.

MRS. JUNO. So you shall, dear. Tell me: do you really like me? I don't mean love me: you might love the housemaid—

GREGORY. [*vehemently.*] No!

MRS. JUNO. Oh, yes you might; and what does that matter, anyhow? Are you really fond of me? Are we friends—comrades? Would you be sorry if I died?

GREGORY. [*shrinking.*] Oh, don't.

MRS. JUNO. Or was it the usual aimless man's lark: a mere shipboard flirtation?

GREGORY. Oh, no, no: nothing half so bad, so vulgar, so wrong. I assure you I only meant to be agreeable. It grew on me before I noticed it.

MRS. JUNO. And you were glad to let it grow?

GREGORY. I let it grow because the board was not up.

MRS. JUNO. Bother the board! I am just as fond of Sibthorpe as—

GREGORY. Sibthorpe!

MRS. JUNO. Sibthorpe is my husband's Christian name. I oughtn't to call him Tops to you now.

GREGORY. [chuckling.] It sounded like something to drink. But I have no right to laugh at him. My Christian name is Gregory, which sounds like a powder.

MRS. JUNO. [chilled.] That is so like a man! I offer you my heart's warmest friendliest feeling; and you think of nothing but a silly joke. A quip like that makes you forget me.

GREGORY. Forget you! Oh, if I only could!

MRS. JUNO. If you could, would you?

GREGORY. [burying his shamed face in his hands.] No: I'd die first. Oh, I hate myself.

MRS. JUNO. I glory in myself. It's so jolly to be reckless. CAN a man be reckless, I wonder.

GREGORY. [straightening himself desperately.] No. I'm not reckless. I know what I'm doing: my conscience is awake. Oh, where is the intoxication of love? the delirium? the madness that makes a man think the world well lost for the woman he adores? I don't think anything of the sort: I see that it's not worth it: I know that it's wrong: I have never in my life been cooler, more businesslike.

MRS. JUNO. [opening her arms to him] But you can't resist me.

GREGORY. I must. I ought [throwing himself into her arms.] Oh, my darling, my treasure, we shall be sorry for this.

MRS. JUNO. We can forgive ourselves. Could we forgive ourselves if we let this moment slip?

GREGORY. I protest to the last. I'm against this. I have been pushed over a precipice. I'm innocent. This wild joy, this exquisite tenderness, this ascent into heaven can thrill me to the uttermost fibre of my heart [with a gesture of ecstasy she hides her face on his shoulder]; but it can't subdue my mind or corrupt my conscience, which still shouts to the skies that I'm not a willing party to this outrageous conduct. I repudiate the bliss with which you are filling me.

MRS. JUNO. Never mind your conscience. Tell me how happy you are.

GREGORY. No, I recall you to your duty. But oh, I will give you my life with both hands if you can tell me that you feel for me one millionth part of what I feel for you now.

MRS. JUNO. Oh, yes, yes. Be satisfied with that. Ask for no more. Let me go.

GREGORY. I can't. I have no will. Something stronger than either of us is in command here. Nothing on earth or in heaven can part us now. You know that, don't you?

MRS. JUNO. Oh, don't make me say it. Of course I know. Nothing—not life nor death nor shame nor anything can part us.

A MATTER-OF-FACT MALE VOICE IN THE CORRIDOR. All right. This must be it.

[The two recover with a violent start; release one another; and spring back to opposite sides of the lounge.]

GREGORY. That did it.

MRS. JUNO. [*in a thrilling whisper*] Sh—sh—sh! That was my husband's voice.

GREGORY. Impossible: it's only our guilty fancy.

A WOMAN'S VOICE. This is the way to the lounge. I know it.

GREGORY. Great Heaven! we're both mad. That's my wife's voice.

MRS. JUNO. Ridiculous! Oh! we're dreaming it all. We [*the door opens; and Sibthorpe Juno appears in the roseate glow of the corridor (which happens to be papered in pink) with Mrs. Lunn, like Tannhauser in the hill of Venus. He is a fussily energetic little man, who gives himself an air of gallantry by greasing the points of his moustaches and dressing very carefully. She is a tall, imposing, handsome, languid woman, with flashing dark eyes and long lashes. They make for the chesterfield, not noticing the two palpitating figures blotted against the walls in the gloom on either side. The figures flit away noiselessly through the window and disappear.*]

JUNO. [*officiously*] Ah: here we are. [*He leads the way to the sofa.*] Sit down: I'm sure you're tired. [*She sits.*] That's right. [*He sits beside her on her left.*] Hullo! [*he rises*] this sofa's quite warm.

MRS. LUNN. [*bored*] Is it? I don't notice it. I expect the sun's been on it.

JUNO. I felt it quite distinctly: I'm more thinly clad than you. [*He sits down again, and proceeds, with a sigh of satisfaction.*] What a relief to get off the ship and have a private room! That's the worst of a ship. You're under observation all the time.

MRS. LUNN. But why not?

JUNO. Well, of course there's no reason: at least I suppose not. But, you know, part of the romance of a journey is that a man keeps imagining that something might happen; and he can't do that if there are a lot of people about and it simply can't happen.

MRS. LUNN. Mr. Juno: romance is all very well on board ship; but when your foot touches the soil of England there's an end of it.

JUNO. No: believe me, that's a foreigner's mistake: we are the most romantic people in the world, we English. Why, my very presence here is a romance.

MRS. LUNN. [*faintly ironical*] Indeed?

JUNO. Yes. You've guessed, of course, that I'm a married man.

MRS. LUNN. Oh, that's all right. I'm a married woman.

JUNO. Thank Heaven for that! To my English mind, passion is not real passion without guilt. I am a red-blooded man, Mrs. Lunn: I can't help it. The tragedy of my life is that I married, when quite young, a woman whom I couldn't help being very fond of. I longed for a guilty passion—for the real thing—the wicked thing; and yet I couldn't care twopence for any other woman when my wife was about. Year after year went by: I felt my youth slipping away without ever having had a romance in my life; for marriage is all very well; but it isn't romance. There's nothing wrong in it, you see.

MRS. LUNN. Poor man! How you must have suffered!

JUNO. No: that was what was so tame about it. I wanted to suffer. You get so sick of being happily married. It's always the happy marriages that break up. At last my wife and I agreed that we ought to take a holiday.

MRS. LUNN. Hadn't you holidays every year?

JUNO. Oh, the seaside and so on! That's not what we meant. We meant a holiday from one another.

MRS. LUNN. How very odd!

JUNO. She said it was an excellent idea; that domestic felicity was making us perfectly idiotic; that she wanted a holiday, too. So we agreed to go round the world in opposite directions. I started for Suez on the day she sailed for New York.

MRS. LUNN. [*suddenly becoming attentive*] That's precisely what Gregory and I did. Now I wonder did he want a holiday from me! What he said was that he wanted the delight of meeting me after a long absence.

JUNO. Could anything be more romantic than that? Would anyone else than an Englishman have thought of it? I daresay my temperament seems tame to your boiling southern blood—

MRS. LUNN. My what!

JUNO. Your southern blood. Don't you remember how you told me, that night in the saloon when I sang "Farewell and adieu to you dear Spanish ladies," that you were by birth a lady of Spain? Your splendid Andalusian beauty speaks for itself.

MRS. LUNN. Stuff! I was born in Gibraltar. My father was Captain Jenkins. In the artillery.

JUNO. [*ardently*] It is climate and not race that determines the temperament. The fiery sun of Spain blazed on your cradle; and it rocked to the roar of British cannon.

MRS. LUNN. What eloquence! It reminds me of my husband when he was in love before we were married. Are you in love?

JUNO. Yes; and with the same woman.

MRS. LUNN. Well, of course, I didn't suppose you were in love with two women.

JUNO. I don't think you quite understand. I meant that I am in love with you.

MRS. LUNN. [*relapsing into deepest boredom*] Oh, that! Men do fall in love with me. They all seem to think me a creature with volcanic passions: I'm sure I don't know why; for all the volcanic women I know are plain little creatures with sandy hair. I don't consider human volcanoes respectable. And I'm so tired of the subject! Our house is always full of women who are in love with my husband and men who are in love with me. We encourage it because it's pleasant to have company.

JUNO. And is your husband as insensible as yourself?

MRS. LUNN. Oh, Gregory's not insensible: very far from it; but I am the only woman in the world for him.

JUNO. But you? Are you really as insensible as you say you are?

MRS. LUNN. I never said anything of the kind. I'm not at all insensible by nature; but (I don't know whether you've noticed it) I am what people call rather a fine figure of a woman.

JUNO. [*passionately*] Noticed it! Oh, Mrs. Lunn! Have I been able to notice anything else since we met?

MRS. LUNN. There you go, like all the rest of them! I ask you, how do you expect a woman to keep up what you call her sensibility when this sort of thing has happened to her about three times a week ever since she was seventeen? It used to upset me and terrify me at first. Then I got rather a taste for it. It came to a climax with Gregory: that was why I married him. Then it became a mild lark, hardly worth the trouble. After that I found it valuable once or twice as a spinal tonic when I was run down; but now it's an unmitigated bore. I don't mind your declaration: I daresay it gives you a certain pleasure to make it. I quite understand that you adore me; but (if you don't mind) I'd rather you didn't keep on saying so.

JUNO. Is there then no hope for me?

MRS. LUNN. Oh, yes. Gregory has an idea that married women keep lists of the men they'll marry if they become widows. I'll put your name down, if that will satisfy you.

JUNO. Is the list a long one?

MRS. LUNN. Do you mean the real list? Not the one I show to Gregory: there are hundreds of names on that; but the little private list that he'd better not see?

JUNO. Oh, will you really put me on that? Say you will.

MRS. LUNN. Well, perhaps I will. [*He kisses her hand.*] Now don't begin abusing the privilege.

JUNO. May I call you by your Christian name?

MRS. LUNN. No: it's too long. You can't go about calling a woman Seraphita.

JUNO. [*ecstatically*] Seraphita!

MRS. LUNN. I used to be called Sally at home; but when I married a man named Lunn, of course that became ridiculous. That's my one little pet joke. Call me Mrs. Lunn for short. And change the subject, or I shall go to sleep.

JUNO. I can't change the subject. For me there is no other subject. Why else have you put me on your list?

MRS. LUNN. Because you're a solicitor. Gregory's a solicitor. I'm accustomed to my husband being a solicitor and telling me things he oughtn't to tell anybody.

JUNO. [*ruefully*] Is that all? Oh, I can't believe that the voice of love has ever thoroughly awakened you.

MRS. LUNN. No: it sends me to sleep. [*Juno appeals against this by an amorous demonstration.*] It's no use, Mr. Juno: I'm hopelessly respectable: the Jenkinses always were. Don't you realize that unless most women were like that, the world couldn't go on as it does?

JUNO. [*darkly*] You think it goes on respectably; but I can tell you as a solicitor—

MRS. LUNN. Stuff! of course all the disreputable people who get into trouble go to you, just as all the sick people go to the doctors; but most people never go to a solicitor.

JUNO. [*rising, with a growing sense of injury*] Look here, Mrs. Lunn: do you think a man's heart is a potato? or a turnip? or a ball of knitting wool? that you can throw it away like this?

MRS. LUNN. I don't throw away balls of knitting wool. A man's heart seems to me much like a sponge: it sops up dirty water as well as clean.

JUNO. I have never been treated like this in my life. Here am I, a married man, with a most attractive wife: a wife I adore, and who adores me, and has never as much as looked at any other man since we were married. I come and throw all this at your feet. I! I, a solicitor! braving the risk of your husband putting me into the divorce court and making me a beggar and an outcast! I do this for your sake. And you go on as if I were making no sacrifice: as if I had told you it's a fine evening, or asked you to have a cup of tea. It's not human. It's not right. Love has its rights as well as respectability [*he sits down again, aloof and sulky.*]

MRS. LUNN. Nonsense! Here, here's a flower [*she gives him one.*] Go and dream over it until you feel hungry. Nothing brings people to their senses like hunger.

JUNO. [*contemplating the flower without rapture*] What good's this?

MRS. LUNN. [*snatching it from him*] Oh! you don't love me a bit.

JUNO. Yes I do. Or at least I did. But I'm an Englishman; and I think you ought to respect the conventions of English life.

MRS. LUNN. But I am respecting them; and you're not.

JUNO. Pardon me. I may be doing wrong; but I'm doing it in a proper and customary manner. You may be doing right; but you're doing it in an unusual and questionable manner. I am not prepared to put up with that. I can stand being badly treated: I'm no baby, and can take care of myself with anybody. And of course I can stand being well treated. But the thing I can't stand is being unexpectedly treated, It's outside my scheme of life. So come now! you've got to behave naturally and straightforwardly with me. You can leave husband and child, home, friends, and country, for my sake, and come with me to some southern isle—or say South America—where we can be all in all to one another. Or you can tell your husband and let him jolly well punch my head if he can. But I'm damned if I'm going to stand any eccentricity. It's not respectable.

GREGORY. [*coming in from the terrace and advancing with dignity to his wife's end of the chesterfield.*] Will you have the goodness, sir, in addressing this lady, to keep your temper and refrain from using profane language?

MRS. LUNN. [*rising, delighted*] Gregory! Darling [*she enfolds him in a copious embrace*]!

JUNO. [*rising*] You make love to another man to my face!

MRS. LUNN. Why, he's my husband.

JUNO. That takes away the last rag of excuse for such conduct. A nice world it would be if married people were to carry on their endearments before everybody!

GREGORY. This is ridiculous. What the devil business is it of yours what passes between my wife and myself? You're not her husband, are you?

JUNO. Not at present; but I'm on the list. I'm her prospective husband: you're only her actual one. I'm the anticipation: you're the disappointment.

MRS. LUNN. Oh, my Gregory is not a disappointment. [*Fondly*] Are you, dear?

GREGORY. You just wait, my pet. I'll settle this chap for you. [*He disengages himself from her embrace, and faces Juno. She sits down placidly.*] You call me a disappointment, do you? Well, I suppose every husband's a disappointment. What about yourself? Don't try to look like an unmarried man. I happen to know the lady you disappointed. I travelled in the same ship with her; and—

JUNO. And you fell in love with her.

GREGORY. [*taken aback*] Who told you that?

JUNO. Aha! you confess it. Well, if you want to know, nobody told me. Everybody falls in love with my wife.

GREGORY. And do you fall in love with everybody's wife?

JUNO. Certainly not. Only with yours.

MRS. LUNN. But what's the good of saying that, Mr. Juno? I'm married to him; and there's an end of it.

JUNO. Not at all. You can get a divorce.

MRS. LUNN. What for?

JUNO. For his misconduct with my wife.

GREGORY. [*deeply indignant*] How dare you, sir, asperse the character of that sweet lady? a lady whom I have taken under my protection.

JUNO. Protection!

MRS. JUNO. [*returning hastily*] Really you must be more careful what you say about me, Mr. Lunn.

JUNO. My precious! [*He embraces her.*] Pardon this betrayal of my feeling; but I've not seen my wife for several weeks; and she is very dear to me.

GREGORY. I call this cheek. Who is making love to his own wife before people now, pray?

MRS. LUNN. Won't you introduce me to your wife, Mr. Juno?

MRS. JUNO. How do you do? [*They shake hands; and Mrs. Juno sits down beside Mrs. Lunn, on her left.*]

MRS. LUNN. I'm so glad to find you do credit to Gregory's taste. I'm naturally rather particular about the women he falls in love with.

JUNO. [*sternly*] This is no way to take your husband's unfaithfulness. [*To Lunn*] You ought to teach your wife better. Where's her feelings? It's scandalous.

GREGORY. What about your own conduct, pray?

JUNO. I don't defend it; and there's an end of the matter.

GREGORY. Well, upon my soul! What difference does your not defending it make?

JUNO. A fundamental difference. To serious people I may appear wicked. I don't defend myself: I am wicked, though not bad at heart. To thoughtless people I may even appear comic. Well, laugh at me: I have given myself away. But Mrs. Lunn seems to have no opinion at all about me. She doesn't seem to know whether I'm wicked or comic. She doesn't seem to care. She has no more sense. I say it's not right. I repeat, I have sinned; and I'm prepared to suffer.

MRS. JUNO. Have you really sinned, Tops?

MRS. LUNN. [*blandly*] I don't remember your sinning. I have a shocking bad memory for trifles; but I think I should remember that—if you mean me.

JUNO. [*raging*] Trifles! I have fallen in love with a monster.

GREGORY. Don't you dare call my wife a monster.

MRS. JUNO. [*rising quickly and coming between them.*] Please don't lose your temper, Mr. Lunn: I won't have my Tops bullied.

GREGORY. Well, then, let him not brag about sinning with my wife. [*He turns impulsively to his wife; makes her rise; and takes her proudly on his arm.*] What pretension has he to any such honor?

JUNO. I sinned in intention. [*Mrs. Juno abandons him and resumes her seat, chilled.*] I'm as guilty as if I had actually sinned. And I insist on being treated as a sinner, and not walked over as if I'd done nothing, by your wife or any other man.

MRS. LUNN. Tush! [*She sits down again contemptuously.*]

JUNO. [*furious*] I won't be belittled.

MRS. LUNN. [*to Mrs. Juno*] I hope you'll come and stay with us now that you and Gregory are such friends, Mrs. Juno.

JUNO. This insane magnanimity—

MRS. LUNN. Don't you think you've said enough, Mr. Juno? This is a matter for two women to settle. Won't you take a stroll on the beach with my Gregory while we talk it over. Gregory is a splendid listener.

JUNO. I don't think any good can come of a conversation between Mr. Lunn and myself. We can hardly be expected to improve one another's morals. [*He passes behind the chesterfield to Mrs. Lunn's end; seizes a chair; deliberately pushes it between Gregory and Mrs. Lunn; and sits down with folded arms, resolved not to budge.*]

GREGORY. Oh! Indeed! Oh, all right. If you come to that—[*he crosses to Mrs. Juno; plants a chair by her side; and sits down with equal determination.*]

JUNO. Now we are both equally guilty.

GREGORY. Pardon me. I'm not guilty.

JUNO. In intention. Don't quibble. You were guilty in intention, as I was.

GREGORY. No. I should rather describe myself guilty in fact, but not in intention.

JUNO. [*rising and exclaiming together*] What!

MRS. JUNO. [*rising and exclaiming together*] No, really—

MRS. LUNN. [*rising and exclaiming together*] Gregory!

GREGORY. Yes: I maintain that I am responsible for my intentions only, and not for reflex actions over which I have no control. [*Mrs. Juno sits down, ashamed.*] I promised my mother that I would never tell a lie, and that I would never make love to a married woman. I never have told a lie—

MRS. LUNN. [*remonstrating*] Gregory! [She sits down again.]

GREGORY. I say never. On many occasions I have resorted to prevarication; but on great occasions I have always told the truth. I regard this as a great occasion; and I won't be intimidated into breaking my promise. I solemnly declare that I did not know until this evening that Mrs. Juno was married. She will bear me out when I say that from that moment my intentions were strictly and resolutely honorable; though my conduct, which I could not control and am therefore not responsible for, was disgraceful—or would have been had this gentleman not walked in and begun making love to my wife under my very nose.

JUNO. [*flinging himself back into his chair*] Well, I like this!

MRS. LUNN. Really, darling, there's no use in the pot calling the kettle black.

GREGORY. When you say darling, may I ask which of us you are addressing?

MRS. LUNN. I really don't know. I'm getting hopelessly confused.

JUNO. Why don't you let my wife say something? I don't think she ought to be thrust into the background like this.

MRS. LUNN. I'm sorry, I'm sure. Please excuse me, dear.

MRS. JUNO. [*thoughtfully*] I don't know what to say. I must think over it. I have always been rather severe on this sort of thing; but when it came to the point I didn't behave as I thought I should behave. I didn't intend to be wicked; but somehow or other, Nature, or whatever you choose to call it, didn't take much notice of my intentions. [*Gregory instinctively seeks her hand and presses it.*] And I really did think, Tops, that I was the only woman in the world for you.

JUNO. [*cheerfully*] Oh, that's all right, my precious. Mrs. Lunn thought she was the only woman in the world for him.

GREGORY. [*reflectively*] So she is, in a sort of a way.

JUNO. [*flaring up*] And so is my wife. Don't you set up to be a better husband than I am; for you're not. I've owned I'm wrong. You haven't.

MRS. LUNN. Are you sorry, Gregory?

GREGORY. [*perplexed*] Sorry?

MRS. LUNN. Yes, sorry. I think it's time for you to say you're sorry, and to make friends with Mr. Juno before we all dine together.

GREGORY. Seraphita: I promised my mother—

MRS. JUNO. [*involuntarily*] Oh, bother your mother! [*Recovering herself*] I beg your pardon.

GREGORY. A promise is a promise. I can't tell a deliberate lie. I know I ought to be sorry; but the flat fact is that I'm not sorry. I find that in this business, somehow or other, there is a disastrous separation between my moral principles and my conduct.

JUNO. There's nothing disastrous about it. It doesn't matter about your principles if your conduct is all right.

GREGORY. Bosh! It doesn't matter about your principles if your conduct is all right.

JUNO. But your conduct isn't all right; and my principles are.

GREGORY. What's the good of your principles being right if they won't work?

JUNO. They will work, sir, if you exercise self-sacrifice.

GREGORY. Oh yes: if, if, if. You know jolly well that self-sacrifice doesn't work either when you really want a thing. How much have you sacrificed yourself, pray?

MRS. LUNN. Oh, a great deal, Gregory. Don't be rude. Mr. Juno is a very nice man: he has been most attentive to me on the voyage.

GREGORY. And Mrs. Juno's a very nice woman. She oughtn't to be; but she is.

JUNO. Why oughtn't she to be a nice woman, pray?

GREGORY. I mean she oughtn't to be nice to me. And you oughtn't to be nice to my wife. And your wife oughtn't to like me. And my wife oughtn't to like you. And if they do, they oughtn't to go on liking us. And I oughtn't to like your wife; and you oughtn't to like mine; and if we do we oughtn't to go on liking them. But we do, all of us. We oughtn't; but we do.

JUNO. But, my dear boy, if we admit we are in the wrong where's the harm of it? We're not perfect; but as long as we keep the ideal before us—

GREGORY. How?

JUNO. By admitting we were wrong.

MRS. LUNN. [springing up, out of patience, and pacing round the lounge intolerantly] Well, really, I must have my dinner. These two men, with their morality, and their promises to their mothers, and their admissions that they were wrong, and their sinning and suffering, and their going on at one another as if it meant anything, or as if it mattered, are getting on my nerves. [Stooping over the back of the chesterfield to address Mrs. Juno] If you will be so very good, my dear, as to take my sentimental husband off my hands occasionally, I shall be more than obliged to you: I'm sure you can stand more male sentimentality than I can. [Sweeping away to the fireplace] I, on my part, will do my best to amuse your excellent husband when you find him tiresome.

JUNO. I call this polyandry.

MRS. LUNN. I wish you wouldn't call innocent things by offensive names, Mr. Juno. What do you call your own conduct?

JUNO. [rising] I tell you I have admitted—

GREGORY. [together] What's the good of keeping on at that?

MRS. JUNO. [together] Oh, not that again, please.

MRS. LUNN. [together] Tops: I'll scream if you say that again.

JUNO. Oh, well, if you won't listen to me—! [He sits down again.]

MRS. JUNO. What is the position now exactly? [Mrs. Lunn shrugs her shoulders and gives up the conundrum. Gregory looks at Juno. Juno turns away his head huffily.] I mean, what are we going to do?

MRS. LUNN. What would you advise, Mr. Juno?

JUNO. I should advise you to divorce your husband.

MRS. LUNN. Do you want me to drag your wife into court and disgrace her?

JUNO. No: I forgot that. Excuse me; but for the moment I thought I was married to you.

GREGORY. I think we had better let bygones be bygones. [To Mrs. Juno, very tenderly] You will forgive me, won't you? Why should you let a moment's forgetfulness embitter all our future life?

MRS. JUNO. But it's Mrs. Lunn who has to forgive you.

GREGORY. Oh, dash it, I forgot. This is getting ridiculous.

MRS. LUNN. I'm getting hungry.

MRS. JUNO. Do you really mind, Mrs. Lunn?

MRS. LUNN. My dear Mrs. Juno, Gregory is one of those terribly uxorious men who ought to have ten wives. If any really nice woman will take him off my hands for a day or two occasionally, I shall be greatly obliged to her.

GREGORY. Seraphita: you cut me to the soul [*he weeps.*]

MRS. LUNN. Serve you right! You'd think it quite proper if it cut me to the soul.

MRS. JUNO. Am I to take Sibthorpe off your hands too, Mrs. Lunn?

JUNO. [*rising*] Do you suppose I'll allow this?

MRS. JUNO. You've admitted that you've done wrong, Tops. What's the use of your allowing or not allowing after that?

JUNO. I do not admit that I have done wrong. I admit that what I did was wrong.

GREGORY. Can you explain the distinction?

JUNO. It's quite plain to anyone but an imbecile. If you tell me I've done something wrong you insult me. But if you say that something that I did is wrong you simply raise a question of morals. I tell you flatly if you say I did anything wrong you will have to fight me. In fact I think we ought to fight anyhow. I don't particularly want to; but I feel that England expects us to.

GREGORY. I won't fight. If you beat me my wife would share my humiliation. If I beat you, she would sympathize with you and loathe me for my brutality.

MRS. LUNN. Not to mention that as we are human beings and not reindeer or barndoor fowl, if two men presumed to fight for us we couldn't decently ever speak to either of them again.

GREGORY. Besides, neither of us could beat the other, as we neither of us know how to fight. We should only blacken each other's eyes and make fools of ourselves.

JUNO. I don't admit that. Every Englishman can use his fists.

GREGORY. You're an Englishman. Can you use yours?

JUNO. I presume so: I never tried.

MRS. JUNO. You never told me you couldn't fight, Tops. I thought you were an accomplished boxer.

JUNO. My precious: I never gave you any ground for such a belief.

MRS. JUNO. You always talked as if it were a matter of course. You spoke with the greatest contempt of men who didn't kick other men downstairs.

JUNO. Well, I can't kick Mr. Lunn downstairs. We're on the ground floor.

MRS. JUNO. You could throw him into the harbor.

GREGORY. Do you want me to be thrown into the harbor?

MRS. JUNO. No: I only want to show Tops that he's making a ghastly fool of himself.

GREGORY. [*rising and prowling disgustedly between the chesterfield and the windows*] We're all making fools of ourselves.

JUNO. [*following him*] Well, if we're not to fight, I must insist at least on your never speaking to my wife again.

GREGORY. Does my speaking to your wife do you any harm?

JUNO. No. But it's the proper course to take. [*Emphatically.*] We MUST behave with some sort of decency.

MRS. LUNN. And are you never going to speak to me again, Mr. Juno?

JUNO. I'm prepared to promise never to do so. I think your husband has a right to demand that. Then if I speak to you after, it will not be his fault. It will be a breach of my promise; and I shall not attempt to defend my conduct.

GREGORY. [*facing him*] I shall talk to your wife as often as she'll let me.

MRS. JUNO. I have no objection to your speaking to me, Mr. Lunn.

JUNO. Then I shall take steps.

GREGORY. What steps?

JUNO. Steps. Measures. Proceedings. What steps as may seem advisable.

MRS. LUNN. [*to Mrs. Juno*] Can your husband afford a scandal, Mrs. Juno?

MRS. JUNO. No.

MRS. LUNN. Neither can mine.

GREGORY. Mrs. Juno: I'm very sorry I let you in for all this. I don't know how it is that we contrive to make feelings like ours, which seems to me to be beautiful and sacred feelings, and which lead to such interesting and exciting adventures, end in vulgar squabbles and degrading scenes.

JUNO. I decline to admit that my conduct has been vulgar or degrading.

GREGORY. I promised—

JUNO. Look here, old chap: I don't say a word against your mother; and I'm sorry she's dead; but really, you know, most women are mothers; and they all die some time or other; yet that doesn't make them infallible authorities on morals, does it?

GREGORY. I was about to say so myself. Let me add that if you do things merely because you think some other fool expects you to do them, and he expects you to do them because he thinks you expect him to expect you to do them, it will end in everybody doing what nobody wants to do, which is in my opinion a silly state of things.

JUNO. Lunn: I love your wife; and that's all about it.

GREGORY. Juno: I love yours. What then?

JUNO. Clearly she must never see you again.

MRS. JUNO. Why not?

JUNO. Why not! My love: I'm surprised at you.

MRS. JUNO. Am I to speak only to men who dislike me?

JUNO. Yes: I think that is, properly speaking, a married woman's duty.

MRS. JUNO. Then I won't do it: that's flat. I like to be liked. I like to be loved. I want everyone round me to love me. I don't want to meet or speak to anyone who doesn't like me.

JUNO. But, my precious, this is the most horrible immorality.

MRS. LUNN. I don't intend to give up meeting you, Mr. Juno. You amuse me very much. I don't like being loved: it bores me. But I do like to be amused.

JUNO. I hope we shall meet very often. But I hope also we shall not defend our conduct.

MRS. JUNO. [*rising*] This is unendurable. We've all been flirting. Need we go on footling about it?

JUNO. [*huffily*] I don't know what you call footling—

MRS. JUNO. [*cutting him short*] You do. You're footling. Mr. Lunn is footling. Can't we admit that we're human and have done with it?

JUNO. I have admitted it all along. I—

MRS. JUNO. [*almost screaming*] Then stop footling.

[*The dinner gong sounds.*]

MRS. LUNN. [*rising*] Thank heaven! Let's go in to dinner. Gregory: take in Mrs. Juno.

GREGORY. But surely I ought to take in our guest, and not my own wife.

MRS. LUNN. Well, Mrs. Juno is not your wife, is she?

GREGORY. Oh, of course: I beg your pardon. I'm hopelessly confused. [*He offers his arm to Mrs. Juno, rather apprehensively.*]

MRS. JUNO. You seem quite afraid of me [*she takes his arm.*]

GREGORY. I am. I simply adore you. [*They go out together; and as they pass through the door he turns and says in a ringing voice to the other couple*] I have said to Mrs. Juno that I simply adore her. [*He takes her out defiantly.*]

MRS. LUNN. [*calling after him*] Yes, dear. She's a darling. [*To Juno*] Now, Sibthorpe.

JUNO. [*giving her his arm gallantly*] You have called me Sibthorpe! Thank you. I think Lunn's conduct fully justifies me in allowing you to do it.

MRS. LUNN. Yes: I think you may let yourself go now.

JUNO. Seraphita: I worship you beyond expression.

MRS. LUNN. Sibthorpe: you amuse me beyond description. Come. [*They go in to dinner together.*]

THE END

CPSIA information can be obtained at www.ICGtesting.com
Printed in the USA
BVOW07s1105280814

364664BV00001B/160/P